conjure

Wobble (2018)

Entanglements (2017)

Partly (2016)

Itself (2015)

Just Saying (2013)

Money Shot (2011)

Versed (2009)

Next Life (2007)

Collected Prose (2007)

Up to Speed (2004)

Veil: New and Selected Poems (2001)

The Pretext (2001)

True (1998)

Made to Seem (1995)

Necromance (1991)

Precedence (1985)

The Invention of Hunger (1979)

Extremities (1978)

conjure

RAE ARMANTROUT

Wesleyan University Press   Middletown, Connecticut

Wesleyan University Press
Middletown CT 06459
www.wesleyan.edu/wespress
2020 © Rae Armantrout
Manufactured in the United States of America
Designed by Mindy Basinger Hill
Typeset in 10/14 point Adobe Caslon Pro

Library of Congress Cataloging-in-Publication Data

Names: Armantrout, Rae, 1947– author.
Title: Conjure / Rae Armantrout.
Description: First. | Middletown, Connecticut : Wesleyan
    University Press, [2020] | Series: Wesleyan poetry | Includes
    bibliographical references. | Summary: "A new book of poems
    by the National Book Critics Circle Award and Pulitzer
    Prize-winner, exploring thought, dialogue, and everyday
    interactions"— Provided by publisher.
Identifiers: LCCN 2020020404 (print)
    LCCN 2020020405 (ebook)
    ISBN 9780819579362 (hardcover)
    ISBN 9780819579973 (paperback)
    ISBN 9780819579379 (ebook)
Subjects: LCGFT: Poetry.
Classification: LCC PS3551.R455 C66 2020 (print)
    LCC PS3551.R455 (ebook)
    DDC 345.73/0243—dc23
LC record available at https://lccn.loc.gov/2020020404
LC ebook record available at https://lccn.loc.gov/2020020405

5 4 3 2 1

CONTENTS

conjure

CONJURE

How did the synthesis
cross the abyss?

In a sentimental story
there is only one

of something:
one newborn,

one moment, one
"once," embalmed

in myrrh.

All I want
is not to be

first on one side,
then the other,

but to conjure
a stream

of sounds and images
for which I am not

responsible.
and maneuver within it—

mouth and tail
one thought.

The sea, now full
of cannibal

jellies, blue
if the sky says so

Take this cup away from me
with its hints

of ammonia and dill,
oak or corrosion.

Who knows, really?

What might ammonia taste like
to a different person?

Roll that question
around on your tongue.

You've heard it before
or something like it.

The familiar is enormous!

Red-shifted.

I'm happy to think
of this deep sleep—

"the sleep of the dead"—

as a guilty pleasure
"I" am

"getting away"
"with"

PINOCCHIO

Strand. String.
In this dream,

the paths cross
and cross again.

They are spelling
a real boy

out of repetition.

Each one
is the one

real boy.

Each knows
he must be

wrong
about this, but

he can't feel
how

The fish
and the fisherman,

the pilot,
the princess,

the fireman and
the ones on fire

TOUCHED

More than a fistful
of stubby green fingers
pushing up through gravel.

And blades, hearts, clubs
cut fine figures too.

Each shape particular
and pushy.

Each a would-be
template,

I say.
Pick me.

I'm with the deranged.
Something's very wrong.

There are masks
in offices.

Machines run the banks
and the power company.

If you *aren't* my mother
or my son,
who are you?

And if you are,
why don't you know me?

FORESIGHT

1

The way we gather
at the window, pointing

with funereal awe

to this thing
that isn't one of us—

a doe
nibbling the lawn.

2

Reflections
staggered by ripples

at the feet
of quaint buildings

in paintings
on hotel-chain walls.

CLIP ART

Stroking her cheek,
I'm drawing

mirror image arcs
in the baby's brain—

closed parentheses
left hanging.

Our topiary space.

PROMOTION

Then the evening
and the morning
were the last day.

But wasn't I promoted
after I named everything?

In cartoons, each
impulse

gets its own
signature shape.

They foil one another
yet remain intact—

static dressed up
as "zany"
or "hectic."

Here is the fur coat
gnawing wears.

Point to its pointed teeth.

THE JOB

Attending to verbal constructs
makes care long-term,
not acute,

which is for the best
because, though flawed,
each one is salvageable

or replaceable
unlike my flesh.
Words can be compared

with moments,
houses, trees, wires
wires, trees, houses.

All stand
on their marks.
Still,

there's a lot of overlap.
I move my eyes
to make time.

I take their measure
and create a duplicate.

SPECULATIVE FICTION

I

The idea that producing a string of nonsense syllables
while pointing toward an object
may cause that object to change
is common in children on the verge of language.

The idea that force exists only
as an interaction between objects
while an object
is a kind of kink
        in a force field.

The idea that, if one survives X number of years,
one will live to see how things "turn out"
or even that things "end well."

2

In the future we will face new problems.

How will we represent the variety of human types
once all the large animals are gone?

As sly as a mother;
as hungry as an orphan?

POSE

So the problem we pose
is how to create an intelligent

                                        agent

and then prevent it
from destroying this world?

"Content monitoring
that required the AI's
intentional states
to be transparent
might not be feasible
for all architectures."

A long green straw
stuck in the ground

with two ears (leaves)
protruding

on either side
at intervals

What we meant
by "listening stations"

and when we began
to mean this.

Perhaps its goal would be
to have "thoughts"
pass through its "head"
so it could record them.

"Preparedness is critical."
"Kiss all hope goodbye."
"A friend wants you to like it."

LIKE

Small white lights
twined around white

dead sticks
under a glass dome

flash—
like getting an idea

was the idea.

   ⁀

Like thinking
I want to fall asleep,

each night coming so soon
after the last,

and hosting a string
of tedious dreams

like trying to get back
to my office.

   ⁀

I head
back in
to clear it
        out,

my head

PHILOSOPHICAL INVESTIGATIONS

1

What are your interests?

I'm interested in the way
interest
creates finitude.

Differently translated,

"in choosing itself,
existing being
closes a circuit."

Now every sixteen seconds,
the engine will pass the brakeman
with his arm always raised
beside the empty station.

2

What do you want to do?

All impulses come
from the gods,
as we know,

and lead god knows where,

though each hero
has her own set
of god-given epithets,

"Insta-bright"
and
"All-dimming"

MY LOVE

1

As love settles briefly
on a houseplant,

a shoe,

and with steady purpose
keeps moving

until it climbs the wall,
the sun

2

They say hate is love
turned sour

because it was unwelcome
where it paused.

More often, love's worn thin

by wrapping itself
around unwieldy things

3

Let our eyelids
lie flat

and spread
like lily pads

beside themselves
on a murky pond

TEST

This is only a test,
I was told often.

⌒

I was trying
to count down
to you.

⌒

Five pointed leaves.

Five-petaled flowers.

Starfish.

⌒

I had been cautioned
not to point.

⌒

Feats of balance
might be the solution.

⌒

Perky sepals
back-combed
around the flower's
sticky note.

GUISES

I come up
again and again

as if from the ground,
as if in a dream,

see that I'm naked
and cover myself

in a likeness,
oh Lord,

"iconic."

As if a pebble
could speak for a cave

about "desire"
from a mile off

DISTRIBUTION

You think category
isn't sexy, isn't
sex. Seems you're wrong.

Don't worry. We have
dozens of them, each revamping
the last. A thing

must be recognizable
in order to be
a thing. After a while

you'll want to introduce
some novelty, but since
it's been a while

this could come off
as desperate.
Don't be mad.

You'd like to punish
the smug, crisply packaged
faux-finite?

We have accessories for that.

THE WIG

As long as—

if—

a Harpo Marx wig

of virtual

adjectives

surrounds each thing:

a giddy frizz
of small round leaves—

why not?—

atop springy stems
rising

from the squat
fused trunks

of bursera
in the window

2

Unclaimed,

expressions form,

unite,

and die back

on an infant's face.

WRONG

Sleep, you demented Scheherazade,
yammering nonsense,

desperate to keep up your yarns
and save yourself

while that righteous king
in the brain

thinks, No,
and I am

disagreeably awake.
My head is thick;

my stomach feels empty
but isn't.

Could I be wrong
about sensations?

What is a thick head anyway
but vacuum

registered as throng.

Ok, you're right.
You be the breast.

An old man worries
about his dead
mother

because she is "very
                              old"

NATURAL HISTORIES

1

Since the irrational
"because I said so"
start,

they'd had their differences:

color that isn't really
color, spin
that isn't spin

because attitude's
best
when it has no content.

Ask a physicist
what "charge" is;

he'll say your question
makes no sense.

2

Word had it
that if they surrendered

their feckless ways

and their lives
with no end,

if they joined up,
they would get a head,

something to speak for them.
The head says:

"I don't want to die";

says

"I am all
alone here."

SPECIES

Join habit to preference;
customize your border.

⌒

In Bruegel's *The Fall of the Angels*
the rebels
become novel life-forms:

a round pink fish
with a brick wall face,

a bird with opened
clam shells
for its wings.

Is that supposed to scare me?

⌒

We use rhino and giraffe
to teach our babies
how to point.

NOTICE

The way a gesture
used to ward off trouble
became cheerful waving.

There was so much looming
and vanishing

to take note of
always;

we felt like play actors

before we knew
what we were about

and after.

⌒

Turns out
the mummy's curse
is real.

You pump thick death
out of the ground
and burn it—

it kills you.

But in all the movies
curses are a cheap
plot trick.

The doofus
who can't read the hieroglyph
dies first

and no one misses him.

Them.

We *were* born yesterday.
We're sorry.

GAINSAYING

A transparent ellipse

with blinking lights
around the edges

and an open mouth
at one end

is extremely serious.

These things don't just happen.

⌒

These things don't just happen.

Trait
blockchain encryption.

A glowing purse
that unlatches
with a snap,

horizontally suspended.

⌒

At around age two
a child will be embarrassed

by her reflection.
This means she is self-conscious.

WHERE WILL YOU SPEND ETERNITY

1

How would you describe a God
who *could* use magic
but doesn't,

who prefers elaborate
widgets and toggles,

seconds toppling
one by one,

the careful recording
of endless instructions?

2

We're riveted
by the Hell Show.

The Devil plays a huckster.
What will he come out with next?

Demons banished for dramatic effect
are brought back to lobby

for poisoning children.
We can't believe

they let us watch.
In fact, they make us.

BEACONS

A fire truck
doing lazy eights

in the concrete gulch
of the L.A. River bed

not private exactly,
not exactly pointless—

beneath a not-quite
gray sky, beyond

the palms' fright wigs
is or is not

beckoning

MOTIVE

Cameras are mounted
on walls. In trees?

We want to believe
the cursory glances
of our young neighbors
have missed us

          entirely.

Imagined verbal adequacy!

We stay in
where contestants
opt to live
onscreen
as they compete
in a war
of all against all
in which each
will and can
explain her motive

GRASP

Is it fair to say
you want the scene described
in as much detail
as possible
as if it were a place
where you could be found
and rescued?

The homeless banter at tables
set out by the supermarket Starbucks.

"Everybody Wants to Rule the World"
drifts from the store's sound system.

One woman sleeps stubbornly
upright—
cradled in her arm,
a bottle of 7-Up.

If to recognize
is to watch yourself

grasp

HUNG

"Fall / in love / with your solitude."
says the Instagram poet
with 1.6 million
followers.

Maybe it was
"Eat your hunger."

You're "excited to see"
how you will withstand
the coming cold and dark.

To withstand.
To hang around.
To hang around
with.
To withdraw.
To wither.

"Who are you talking to?"

To this vine
hung with wrinkled
purple bladders.

TELLING

1

I live as if
an angry woman
were shouting, "Say something!"

2

Edges
of the vine-leaves

had a pink tinge,
a trick of the eye

one of us thought,
but we came back

to fully formed, hot pink
cup-husks

each one
with two yellow

eyes, protruding
on thin stalks

So this was
"the fullness of time."

3

We produce ourselves
by reading scripts

on current happenings.

(There is no telling
where I leave off

EXPLANATION

It is a great relief
the way convictions

blossom
and wither

in fast forward
as we sleep.

Like bugs
that walk on water,

we live on the surface
tension

where past
and future meet.

Their friction
is our speech.

WARDROBE

Thread-like formations:
bound galaxies,

fringing
large voids.

Foxgloves grow wild
beside freeways—

pink, speckled,
empty

sleeve upon sleeve.

Nature, you gorgeous
old queen,

your posture
is still perfect.

A ragged web

of galactic
"filaments"

left hanging

CONCEPT

He would spin
until he shone,

until he shone
and exploded.

Then he'd suck it up
and start over.

That was his big idea—
his pleasure.

They called it "stimming"
for "self-stimulation."

But they weren't real.

"That's enough!" they said.

(Enough for proof
of concept)

INTERCEPTS

In the dark, it
wired itself
for light,

numb, it wired itself
for touch

and waited.

Did it wait?

Could it sense time pass?

Only when her limbs moved
did she become aware
of the surrounding medium,

but when did these
become *her*
limbs?

Self-

interested and

intertwined like

dodder

with oak,

dodder known

as witch's hair.

How was this *her*
awareness?

So that each
was now infuriated
by any interaction
with the other
that altered his
or her trajectory,
producing a pause
or swerve.

Was one term
better than another?

And when she tried handing him a sheet of waste paper
because he was standing near the recycle bin, he flinched.

MINE

It's not that each baby wants

what the other has,

it's that each is drawn

to the new focus

of attention

because attention is life,

which they sense

as they careen,

as it careens,

wildly,

deflected by surfaces.

This buzz, this tickle
could be contentment.

Identical
photons jostle.

Even displacement
feels pleasant.

Too faded to identify,
a flag

snaps to attention

on a pole dwarfed
by large cedars.

I whisper "milieu"
as I pull

a cup
from the cupboard.

A human
can surprise herself.

Short phrases stray
to different ends,

begin again
from the same spot:

strings of companion
interims

that music makes
because life won't—

                or won't quite.

PERSISTENCE

You're a person
the way a whirlpool

is a mood
of water's, a certain

inwardness,

a hard suck
on nothing

that pulls itself
erect

"I am that I am,"
God says,

meaning existence
is tautology.

Don't ask.

CAPTURE

1

The brain causes lights
to wink,

to appear
to chase one another

around a small tree
in order

to see itself
reflected?

2

Slow up
and a sense

of importance
attaches,

a lump
in the throat:

matter.

3

Tell us again
what we are:

foxes, stars, mice,
cars,

splotches
of color

captured

CAN YOU SEE

1

Flag lolling
on its pole
like a dog's tongue.

Start over.

Flag lolling
lewdly
on its pole,

then getting up,
sending ripples

through pupils,
wanton.

Is that what you'd say
you saw,

what traipsed through,
careless,

bouncing off the walls?

2

If I'm sure of anything
it's that I'm a spot

between tart and orange
(taut and rough).

I'm where they first touched—
though they don't

touch. They align.
I'm a chimera

factory.

PIECE

What is a brand?
The hopeful tag

on the tan underpants
that reads, "Metaphor"

leaves everything
to the imagination

which by now
is plainly exhausted.

I could describe these tags
as so many

flapping tongues,
dropping hints

about a foreign designer,
himself largely a cover story.

Someone somewhere must sew a shirt
made entirely of red flags.

Untiring, music
rises
then falls through
its imagined past.

PORTRAIT

Have you matched feelings
with images

in order to feel
otherwise?

⌒

The gas fireplace thuds on.

Soon there are small flames
standing beside taller ones,

family groups
at intervals

along winding
ember trails.

⌒

Did you bury
feeling in words

in order to
leave it behind?

⌒

The trails could be lava flows,

strings of small villages
burning.

It's a scene
in which refugees

flicker and subside.

ENCLOSURES

Human interest:

"Patrolling the border
on four legs."

On a plane's silent screen
a clothed moose and baboon
visit an aquarium
where the fish are nude
albeit fluorescent pink.

This film's meant to help kids
identify rare animals
or it's meant
to normalize captivity.

But the glass breaks
and the couple is swept out
onto the street
where a grave koala
addresses survivors
from a mound of wreckage.

Is this a joke?

My account is frozen
And I wake up cold.

Skulls
of all sizes
on his shirt, a parrot
on his arm, a man shuffles
into a supermarket

TANDEM

Where is the link
between kindling
and kin?

I start with second thoughts
and work backwards

toward infantile amnesia.
In the beginning,

there was cremation. No,
in the beginning was a tandem

jiggling of fields.
I sort of liked it.

Mostly I wanted to know
what *else*

was in that bag—
like it was bottomless,

if I'm like you.

2

It seems possible to know
that if I look out back
I will see the intense red
of the rose (lush? deep?)
not as if for the first time
but as if for the first time
truly

and further that each
unfolding, each collapse
will bring with it,
like a booby prize
this same sense of discovery.

3

These streets are called arterials.

For hours
a man grimaces
at traffic

with the "merely formal
purposiveness"

of which Kant speaks.

ABOVE

1

The brain has powerful filters
that screen out most
thoughts and images:

below, a crowded platform,
passengers jostling;

above, an empty stage,
eerie silence in the hall

2

River, even your
one-track mind
looks better
combed to ribbons
over rocks.

Sparrow pivots
left then right
and back—a nervous
shrug.

3

Reader, will you die
bitter?

You were taught
that time's
divisible,

that someone
would pick you up
when you cried.

THE NEW ECONOMY

Creative Souls Cloud City Vape Works.

If, as Rovelli says, there are no
separate things, "only relations"

between the hardly real
and the barely there,

spots where
apprehension tangles

He keeps busy.

He makes
kimonos
for babies
out of cowboy shirts.

CARE

Dress like you care!
Eat like you care!
Care like you care!

You don't think
apples just grow on trees,
do you?

A fish taps a clam
against a bony knob
of coral
to crack its shell—

which demonstrates intelligence
yes, but
is the fish
pleased with itself?

Alone in your crib,
you form syllables.

Are you happy when one
is like another?

Add yourself
to yourself.

Now you have someone

CONTINGENCIES

"Contingent," which comes
from touch,

now means alongside
and by chance.

⌒

Two women asleep
in a supermarket deli,
People magazine between them.

⌒

"Askance," which once meant
from the side,
and now means
with suspicion.

⌒

This Xmas beware
of toys
collecting data, dolls
asking personal questions.

PROBE

No lie!
Need input!
Not ghosting you!
Which coffee is best for wildlife?

Are you going to get the monkey?
Are you taking him to sister?
No, you're giving him to granddad.

Everything we did
was tracked

by sentences.

Now we can't stop
talking to ourselves.

Worried about what happens.

Just need a minute.

We are all
rooting for you.

NEW DEVELOPMENTS

Pine trunks touched
by the same wind
almost feel it.

We invented sex
and violence

because our systems
needed content,

something to deliver,

something that could cross
the gaps.

You think I have that backwards?

We press spine to spine
and our captive
glow-worms chatter.

What do you think they're
going on about?

When we were simpler,
we spoke with others.

"Are you there?" we asked
cell to cell.

Now we're mostly
talking to ourselves.

THE RUNAROUND

I

We encountered a problem

sending
a command

to the program.

Did *I* say that
aloud?

I've broken out
in imps.

To be a blip
in a circuit

and to know it,
to relish

this knowledge
in your private

moments
as all moments

are gated
and switched.

2

When I mentioned hatred
I was not thinking

                              of you,

but you'd best not break
our momentum,

the thrill we get
from our own self-
loathing,

that guilty snigger
running round the room

GHOST STORY

1

A good dream convinces me
the machine can run
unattended
but, in this one, I'm allowed,
no, required
to inspect each scene
for narrative plausibility.

Should I believe that this black paste
made from the souls of the dead
and which I've been rubbing
around on my palate
is normally deposited
by the tongues of frogs
on reeds?

2

The need to factor out
the effects
of one's own movements
on the size and shape
of objects

leaves a silhouette.

FALSE STARTS

1

Because they were never infants,
helpless and speechless
in a world of words,
Adam and Eve are innocent.

End of story.
Start again.

2

From the start,
we notice one another
and become attuned.

We synchronize our movements
as if we wanted to be one

creature which, of course,
we don't.

This is joy.

Even the park trees
imitate us.

OUR HISTORY

1

Before the show begins, there's an ad for enlistment.
"We make the sham solidarity of youth real!"

And this is the heaven we wanted,
starting off together at dawn,
open savannah before us.

Then history.

2

Like tourists, we're taken
by the web of light and shadow
on our wall
and grab our cameras.

Like tourists, we're carried away
by the sober thuds
of *Frontline*'s theme music, its
rhythmically punctuated threats.

3

When I say, "Where have you been?"
I'm furious
because I don't already know.

Are you still,
still
the gap
in my world?

THE REACH

for Renee and Sasha

Now is born again.

Demanding as always,
more sensitive than belief.

She is reckoning the distance
from what is not yet
quite herself

to

no one can tell her
what's dissolving.

But now it's David, now it's Kathy,
now it's Tom.

She doesn't speak our language.

She does not mean it.
She does not mean she.

She is sending out runners or
putting out feelers.

We have manufactured animals
for her to reach.

Was this what she wanted?

PROJECT

Your clock's been turned to zero,
though there is no zero on a clock.
Your skin is petal-soft no matter
how old the starter-kit was—
but you will get tired or bored.
That's when the clock starts up.

Your parents want you happy,
but we also want to set you down,
to get back to our old lives.
How will you turn against us
once you figure this out?

You're about to discover intention.
There are four stuffed animals
in front of you on strings.
They are targets.
You won't understand this for a while.
You flail your arms.
Sometimes you make one bounce.

Are humans the only creatures
who must learn
to move with purpose?
Is that why we harp on motive,
why we think of earth
as some god's handiwork?

FOSSILS

A raven marches straight down
that pitched roof
as if on a mission.

Intention
in birds or babies
seems amusing

The guy walking down the main drag with his pack and bedroll
has a clear purpose—to find someplace
more protected and claim it
before nightfall.

Not that I envy him;
I don't mean that.

I mean that the notions of my neighbors
in these spruced-up or dilapidated houses
with their garden gnomes, stubby windmills,
and crosses
are the fossilized remains
of his quest.

MY HOUSE

A vine drapes the fence
in its cool enthusiasm,

stemmed cascade.
My skin

has collapsed in flounces,
in anticipation.

Look how I change the subject
without changing,

I appear to say—
which seems like nothing

but is practice
for the bigger change
to come.

My mind is just
like the stance

and disposition of these trees—

dense, sparse, conical,
lopsided, frilly

(as was the mind
of the tenant before me

THEATER

Neurons—each of which speaks
only to the same few
neurons its whole life
in the same few words—
confabulate together
a kingpin
acting for them,
hearing everything.

2

The man in the dream
choking on popcorn
insists, "I can't
breathe!" which the crowd
finds unconvincing.
"I've heard *that* before,"
somebody quips.

But where were we?

PARALLAX

The first value is focus.
Then balance.

Backward and forward
offset.

Tat for tat—
just so, as if.

These phantom limbs
go parallax.

"Make something of your life."
Something inanimate.

CROSS OVER

Clang of chimes; bright leaves
shiver with delight.

Where the wires cross—
insights. I want more.

A creek is torn
by rocks

and the wind sends notes
this way and back.

Start in the middle
(everywhere)

and count

WITH US

With us, it's about
choices.

How many kinds
of Kind bars
will we want?

An abandoned pillow
in dry grass

says enough,
but not too much.

It might be a poem.

In our thrillers,
a protagonist
must be convinced
that events concern her.

Could she be involved?

With us, it's about
blast radius.

Maple-pecan is
burnt-ocher

and sand

FLIP THE SCRIPT

Samsung says
the launch codes

are in your twin's heart
but, with his permission,

you will cut them out
and turn the key.

It's the only way
to reach the finale

which, by now, is all
anybody wants

Someone says to be conscious
is to answer
your own questions

without really hearing them—

the way a tower answers
a cell phone's ping.

Now Mobile suggests
you "script the flip,"

rethink the meaning
of tumbling

so that you spin
in thick air,

perhaps grabbing on

to a rope
with your teeth.

We must have asked ourselves,
"What's wrong?"

WORK SONGS

"The Emperor's a Pig
and So Are You,"
starts up again.

It's called freedom.
In a song,

I turn my power on
and prove it all night

and every day
I am defiant

and insulated

in the thought bubble
of your car.

I will survive
is my most popular

moment.

People shoot people. Men
shoot girls

over a stretch
of road

that they don't want,
that they hate.

I've still got
a lot of fight left

MESSAGING

"Entanglement" means two
who have made contact
stay linked
over any distance
so that,
like a couple
in a bad marriage,
if one says "up"
the other will say "down."

A city of conifers,
branches stacked
like discs,
topknots cocked
this way and that, millions
of wry asides,
but who is there
to count?

In the battered
post office, a clerk
with a purple turban,
mustache curled
in two perfect
circles, asks
if he can help.

TURN

Even when not
searching for help
the eye turns
from yellow
tree to tree
in November.

The long, naked
gaze between old
woman and infant
is whole,
real as anything
will be now,
she thinks,
though she knows
the child won't remember
this, will barely
remember her.

A locked gaze
is immersion;
she feels herself floating.
But now the baby
squirms.

SCREEN MEMORY

A branching pattern
is a tracery.

My screen claims
I have "new memories."

A trained vine, splitting,
spitting out white flowers.

A nation of costumed
reenactors

with axes to grind.

THE TOWER

In what they let us see
as a role,

the superhero,
says bitterly,

"My whole life is a lie!"
and it's moving

because it's true.
He's sickened by the weight

of all he's been asked
to defend.

We know how that is,
but now a woman

or a child is dangled
from an office tower

and we're pulled in.

The villain is a symbolist.
He dangles someone

to demonstrate
how precarious our lives are

here.
No one wants to see this,

least of all the superhero,
now fully back in character.

Sign in car window:

It's
not about
us, it's
about Him.

Hot potato.

Of course, it's terrible
when civilians

burn,
when they strangle.

Everyone
will say the same thing.

I'm not lonely
because I have secrets;

I'm lonely because words
can't bring the past
into the present

(which amounts to the same thing).

Jack Rabbit
and the Lonely Present

is the title of a book
I almost wrote

I'm lonely because
you're sure you've heard
something like this
everywhere before.

Polly Pea Pod
and the Deep Hole

You think you can make
something out of it

the way you made much
of the slanted light
and deep shadows
of autumn.

SEVER

1

The peculiar pallor
of the sky at dusk;

the ghost of meaning
in a phrase
often repeated.

2

Critics rave, *Annihilation*
is a haunting
achievement.

3

When severed, do pieces
search each other out?

4

Worms—busy
as fingers—

and they say we can't
tickle ourselves.

STRUCTURES

I

These outsized windows
on either side of a door—
probably new and Plexiglas—
overlooking a freeway,
their wide-eyed expression
sad
in the way it suggests optimism
but is really
the product of an architectural fad
already hardening into habit.

2

For a moment, each poem is a new door
opening in a wall,

but then the hallway it leads to
seems familiar
as does the eeriness of recognition.

I look up to see leaves, thronged at the window,
lambent,
and think maybe there

FRAME

Why are the bare twigs in the window,
clouds inching between their knuckles,
worth watching?

 "Wanting more from the day
is a form
of greed," you said—

or maybe "grief."

Two clouds separate so slowly that, at first, it could be
an illusion. Yet, within minutes, the smaller disappears
beyond the frame's horizon,
leaving no room for doubt.

ALTERNATES

In English we say "through
with"

as if
even in rejection
we would be accompanied.

The mind is a body
double.

In dreams (as in heaven?)
we are never old.

What troubles you?

The way one thing
leads to another

down an access road.

Nonstop wavelets—
yes or no?

OUR REASONS

It's not vacuum

but a welter

of virtual occasions

that comes between you

and the thing

you thought

you

⌒

The eagerness with which
the empty skins
of soap bubbles
adhere, sharing
"a common wall."

⌒

Efficiency suites.

⌒

Keyhole, buttonhole, push button?

Alarm
is loading, please

wait.

⌒

The mind in the dream,
though one of its creatures,
may sometimes be incredulous,

may think this
can't be happening

EVIDENCE

On Sundays crowds would comb through thrift shops
stunned by all that had been, evidently, intended

The ceramic seal,
head craned to stare
at a geranium
protruding from its back.

"Use the Crown Club Card
to see Justice League,"
he, she, it says.

⌒

Let the Mona Lisa stand
for private jokes,

passing thoughts, all
you never knew

about your parents.
Rope her off.

You've done that?
What about the rest?

⌒

I drift off
during ancient mega-floods
scouring the scablands.

⌒

New genre:
the faux selfie-shot,
frozen mugging
for no camera.

HOLDING PATTERNS

1

Holding any pose
is a pain numbed
by long habit.

In this way,
I am sister
to the ridged gourd
and the cracked, wooden
cabinet.

But what of the dog
full of mild
reproach?

2

"Unlike many of us,
no one
has seen anything
like what's going on
right now,"

you say to the cameras
you've managed to capture.

If this were your last thought,
how long could you
hang on to it

before you saw
that it was holding
you

in its
weak fist?

Reindeer pull a sleigh
(through early spring thaw)
on the roof
of the True North
Nail Salon

Signed turnout
where tourists take snapshots
of the pipeline, elevated
on small plinths,
amid scattered birch

Aurora's green sky
gives the mind
what it thinks
it wants: a different
nature, a new world

And notes
of a wind chime—

dissonant, rounded—

Nabokov's "nymphets"
fleeting in place

NONESUCH

This eucalyptus,
with its elliptical leaves

dangling, light and dry
as an abandoned chrysalis,

with its modest bunches
of pale pink flowers

and languid pose,
is my unattainable ideal.

Of a piece,
in pieces,

past it all
and in plain view—

nowhere
in the blasted web

of stars

is there any
such beauty.

PREVIEW

1

There are worldwide, catastrophic storms
when earth's network
of weather-control satellites
is sabotaged by unknown enemies.

As fire rages through the western forest
Jeff Bridges snarls,
"If you want a piece of me,
come get me."

2

The baby says, "Mmm, mmm!"
to the stuffed fish
then hits it
against her closed mouth.

"Ah, ah," she says,
holding it at a distance.

She opens and closes
the palm of one hand. "Bye-bye,"
we say for her.
"Bye-bye, Fishy!"

THE CORNER

Like a child, mind
wants to play, but
even the butterflies
are on the clock.

Still, attention is happy
to comport
with the swallowtail
as it jerkily
rounds the corner.

Like a child, mind
follows, imitates.
First and last
it loves sequence.

I've counted up
to one this season.

TWICE

Just where,
just as

an illegible graph
of bare sticks

marked time
knuckled by knuckle,

hydra-headed
white flowers

on limber wands

throng
the bright window.

As a moment
is a gizmo,

a contraption
for recording coincidence,

a child's toe
is a caught pig

going to market.

I'd give my life for this
flimflam

without thinking
once.

HIDDEN

Thick clouds: a blindfold,
a blanket.

It's called "cozy season."

That autumn and sunset
are beautiful
is poor preparation
for death.

One tree half green, half dusky
red.

Not quite darling.
Not quite "opposites attract."

2

Once we're hidden,
they face each other.

First one then the other
flaps her arms.

First one then the other
bends forward.

One cocks her head
Both laugh.

DRIFT

I

He says it's natural
I should feel abandoned
given that

He doesn't say we're all abandoned
by the past
and by the future.

2

An armored dragonfly drifts
from tree to tree and back
all afternoon

the way I walk into a room
and pause,
not knowing what I came for

JACKPOT

Magic's the art
of misdirection. No,
that's *money*.

"Let your children go
to the movies,"
the poet said,

but what about this:
a troupe of magicians
expose bank fraud

and universal digital surveillance
as the work of one
father-son duo

long believed dead,
but, actually, holed up
in a casino

in Macao?

Entertainment's pricey now.

But you are worth your weight
in cherry-hibiscus gummy

pandas

EVEN

First they thought
they could get things
straight.

Then they thought
they could get
even.

They invented numbers
to find out

if the harm
they'd suffered

equaled the harm
they'd caused.

It didn't.

Then they cast blame
into bars

and carried it
forward.

They were forward looking.
We are.

Numbers tick upward
on a board
above our heads.

We've lost track
of what they measure,

but it's something bad.

SUBJECT RHYMES

Hidden in once dull
office parks

(everywhere)

are nests of spies
and malware coders,

high on security clearance
like debauched celebs

at the fabled clubs
people just *died*

to get into
but couldn't.

Tenfold is nothing
to the new

digital
with its near limitless

fingerings

(cloaked in vestigial
metaphor),

its fugue state
buzz.

The bit
where the two

ends
find each other

in all their mysterious
"each otherness":

popcorn

In the wicker chair (for sale)
at One World Market,
an old homeless man, slumped
so his head rests
on his knees,

and across from him,
a plump, bored kid
in Bermuda shorts
waiting

The man rushing past
calling out body measurements,
"5'10", 180 pounds. Oh yeah!"
in a voice full of anger

To stroke
the dream's fur
beside the dream's hearth
is happiness

even as I see
that this is not
my cat, that I am
not myself

EXECUTION

The way
a new blade
steadies itself
as it slowly
unfurls.

It's not glazed
doughnuts or

it is.

Gray and silver
bellies
of clouds, sun-slit.

Power lines swooping
out and in. Ridiculous.

"People are happy
when their lives have purpose,"

some plan
to execute.

FUNNEL

Target a high
value audience low

in the purchasing
funnel.

                    Coke

has always been about
inclusion

TWILIGHT

Where there's smoke
there are mirrors

and a dry-ice machine,
industrial quality fans.

If I've learned anything
about the present moment

⁓

But who doesn't
love a flame,

the way one leaps
into being

full-fledged,
then leans over

to chat

⁓

Already the light
is retrospective,
sourceless,

is losing itself
though the trees
are clearly limned.

OLD TRICKS

For light
so loved
the light
that it kindled
what it touched
and answered itself
wherever it went.

Now the lightning strike
of the chameleon
and the hard eye
of the blue-black bug
it's swallowing.

All tricks
of the light—
old favorites,
new kinks.

From a bathtub
each night
let crickets sing.

MADE SHORT

1

Like us, the quanta
spend most of their time

in limbo

where time isn't
theirs

and there is nothing
to acquire

until nothing
sends them flying

and they get
realized.

2

In impact studies, crash
courses, tell-alls.

3

In the dream,
I was led to believe
that memorabilia
would fill the canyon, rubble
I could walk across
unharmed

VERSIONS

Everything is made
of yes and no.
Or everything is made
of simple
particles,
which are made
of impulse,
which is
made of nothing

yet

Here are the penguin, the sloth,
the skink,

all forms
of exaggeration.

Dinner-plate dahlias
profuse as if

there were no end

to concentric
orange ruffles.

2

A human holds
that what survives her death
is the direction
of her gaze.

THE HEDGE

Unlikely,
the home life

of water
on fire.

⌒

Love doubling love's
approximations.

⌒

Unlikely, its
nucleated quirks.

Ice rinks in malls
in warm climates.

⌒

These rolling carts, these registers
that chirp, "Did you find
everything you needed?"

⌒

Your lives
are getting heavy.

You hedge your
breath,

you think

CLOSER

The critics say
we've finally begun to move
from solipsism
to futility.

It's true
that standing still
is exhausting.

As a way out
of myself
(and into someone near me),

more gripping
than vampire stories,
more realistic
than falling in love,

I watch toddlers
form thoughts
and act on them.

BREATH

1

Let's say
a child takes
each bow
from a bag of bows
eagerly,
placing it on the carpet
after brief inspection,
and has just begun
putting them back in
one by one
when a second person

2

Let's say
dilatory nomenclature,

nylon bikini briefs,
light breeze,

churn
of chopper blades—

how many yards above me?—

bearing down,
then rising

into irrelevance.
But what isn't

someone's metaphor?

3

Calcium ion transport.

All the bows are made of oil.

All the container ships
have names.

UNDERSTANDINGS

To convey great effort
and mild reluctance,
one groans briefly
when sitting up in bed.

This is sometimes known
as prayer.

Ignore the wind chimes.
They're a bad example.

To stand beneath
or walk behind—

to comprehend!—

to grab wildly
at surrounding objects.

Some grab at attention
by quipping, "I don't care."

Others sit in corners
closely watching their fingers.

We fill the world
with selfie avatars,

and more and more
children

refuse to recognize their names.

MY POINT

I

A lake's hither
and here,

its pearly indecision
and mysterious clear spot.

Its drifting skein
of small worries

is one way
of being at peace.

2

To arrive at this
can't have been easy:

this oval, wafer body,
flat, yellow eyes
on either side of what
should not be called a nose,
but is, rather,
the point you make
to provide yourself
with direction
as you shrug,
glide, shrug, glide
around your tank,

your form
arcane and ecstatic.

3

Let's play a game.

What do a fish and a lake
have in common?

Nothing!

A lake
is a reflective state,

while a fish
is somebody.

VALUE ADDED

The way orchid
splits the difference

with hot pink,
say,

in the hanging
plastic crystal—

how an increased level
of saturation

can come across
as reticence

or even
as retraction.

There, where it changes
tack—

the *as* in the
"come across as"—

put your tongue on that.

THE CONVERSATION

I

They make a difference.
They fluoresce.

They answer
the blue light

that reaches them
           here

by stretching
its wavelength, glowing

red, yellow, green

2

If any liquid
in a paper cup

were known as
"Love Your Beverage"

a disturbing commandment
would be lifted

and we wouldn't face
the hard problem

of deciding who
is addressing whom

PUPIL

1

Drawn to a lodestone,
your attention

is collapsing,
pouring

through a hole,
a point

which is nothing
compounded

until all else
breaks loose.

2

The puma sits behind
her own eyes
only—

so some say
she has no mind

PETARD

We hoped to see things as they are
by which we meant without us.

We thought once we stripped away
smell, taste, color—

anything improper—

leaving only location
and number,

the thing
would be naked

on the teeter-totter
of an equation.

2

Then Archimedes
told another one.

If I had a long enough lever
and a fulcrum,

I'd get a high
resolution image

of objectified bodies
and hoist myself

on my own petard.

PLANULAR

Whether fission
is accompanied
by pleasure
is an open
maw.

Fertilization occurs
either in the gastro-
vascular cavity
or in the water column
itself.

The most rigorous practice
can resemble indifference.

Larvae
wriggle free
and drift
with the currents

COSTUMES

Man in pirate get-up,
slumped
in a folding chair
on a corner
by the on-ramp—

half seen by drivers
angling for position.

On the seventh day, we rested
surrounded by lakes
of pig effluent, dunes
of coal ash. By that time,
it was late summer.
Soon we would scare ourselves
a little
and give thanks.

Just when we were sick
of our appetites, our choices
the children came along
and presented them
in miniature—

not as monsters,
but as pets
we'd want to feed.

THE REST

1

On the eighth day,
he started again,

doing math in his head,

dividing light
by darkness.

Doing meth in bed
is messed up,

but we haven't reached
that juncture yet

2

How like a flamenco dancer
who never tires

of drama,

this twisted
bougainvillea, climbing

at the window,
pouting forth

its pink lips.

But why should I go
and spoil everything?

NOW SEE

Don't worry.

We have armies
of showrunners

writing our dreams,
ones where we're featured

as skilled apparatchiks
facing credible threats

that appear and disappear
like clockwork,

leaving no apparent
damage.

2

It was all one
to me—

all pain-pleasure,
all squirmy

life-death
until your head

broke the surface
and looked

backward and forward.
Now see

what you've done.

ACKNOWLEDGMENTS

The author wants to thank the editors of the following journals
and anthologies:

Academy of American Poets' Poem-a Day, *The American Journal of
Poetry*, Berkeley Art Museum Way Bay 2 Postcard Series, *Conjunctions*,
CounterText, *The Elephant*, *The Equalizer*, *Golden Handcuffs*, *Granta*
online, *Hambone*, *Harper's*, *Harvard Review*, *Have Your Chill*, *Interim*,
Inverted Syntax, *Jacket2*, *The Journal*, *Journal of Poetic Research*, *Juxtaprose*,
The Kenyon Review, *Lana Turner*, *The London Review of Books*,
The Los Angeles Review of Books, *The New Yorker*, *The Paris Review*,
Plume, *Poetry*, *Posit*, sfu Chapbook Series, *Touch the Donkey*, *Vallum*,
Wave Composition, *West Branch*, *Women's Review of Books*, *X-Peri*

The Body in Language: An Anthology (Counterpath, 2019)

Plume Poetry 7 (Canisy Press, 2019)

Watch Your Head (Coach House Press, forthcoming)

Rae Armantrout is professor emerita of writing at the University of California, San Diego. She has published fifteen books of poetry and been featured in a number of major anthologies. Her book *Versed*, published by Wesleyan University Press, won the 2009 National Book Critics Circle Award and the 2010 Pulitzer Prize for Poetry. Armantrout's recent collections include *Wobble* (a finalist for the 2018 National Book Award), *Entanglements* (2017), *Partly: New and Selected Poems, 2001–2015* (2016), *Itself* (2015), and *Just Saying* (2013), all published by Wesleyan University Press. She is the recipient of numerous other awards, including an award in poetry from the Foundation for Contemporary Arts in 2007 and a Guggenheim Fellowship in 2008.